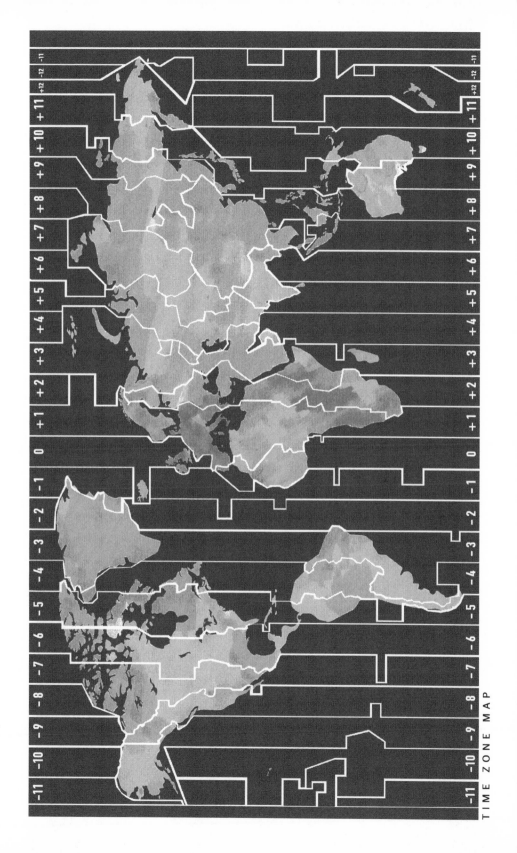

TIME ZONE MAP

DESTINATION(S):

GOOD TO KNOW ABOUT REGION AND CULTURE:

# PACKING LIST

## TO DO BEFORE LEAVING

# BUCKET LIST

# BUDGET

|  |  |
|---|---|
|  |  |

| | | | | | | | | | | | | | |
|---|---|---|---|---|---|---|---|---|---|---|---|---|---|

TOTAL: | TOTAL:

LOCATION:                                          DATE:

LOCATION:                              DATE:

LOCATION:                                          DATE:

DESTINATION(S):

GOOD TO KNOW ABOUT REGION AND CULTURE:

# PACKING LIST

## TO DO BEFORE LEAVING

# BUCKET LIST

- [ ]
- [ ]
- [ ]
- [ ]
- [ ]
- [ ]
- [ ]
- [ ]
- [ ]
- [ ]
- [ ]
- [ ]
- [ ]
- [ ]
- [ ]
- [ ]
- [ ]
- [ ]
- [ ]
- [ ]
- [ ]
- [ ]
- [ ]
- [ ]
- [ ]
- [ ]
- [ ]
- [ ]
- [ ]
- [ ]
- [ ]
- [ ]

# BUDGET

|  |  |  |  |  |  |  |  |  |  |
|---|---|---|---|---|---|---|---|---|---|

TOTAL:          TOTAL:

LOCATION:                                          DATE:

LOCATION:                                          DATE:

LOCATION:                                    DATE:

LOCATION:                                          DATE:

LOCATION:                                    DATE:

LOCATION:                          DATE:

LOCATION:                                          DATE:

LOCATION:                                    DATE: